young CHANGEMAKERS

INSPIRING OTHERS

Written By
STACY C. BAUER

Illustrated By
EMANUELA NTAMACK

For Aly, C.J., Asher, Sharleen, Ada, Anabelle, Nate, Clara, Ian, Livy, Padraig, Christian, Ryan, Brynley and Zuriel. Thank you for allowing me to share your amazing stories with the world. Keep changing lives.

Inspiring Others
Young Change Makers
Published by Hop Off the Press, LLC
www.stacycbauer.com

Minneapolis, MN

Book design by Travis D. Peterson.

Library of Congress Control Number: 2021913717
Bauer, Stacy C. Author
Ntamack, Emanuela Illustrator
Inspiring Others

ISBN: 978-1-7373890-6-4

JUVENILE NONFICTION

Printed in China.

All inquiries of this book can be sent to the author.
For more information, please visit **www.stacycbauer.com**

MEET THE
CHANGE MAKERS!

 **HELPING HANDS**
Delivering support to those in need.

ANIMAL AMBASSADORS
Helping and advocating for animals.

INSPIRATIONAL ICONS
Chasing their dreams and
encouraging others to do the same!

CONSERVATION CREW
Saving the planet.

BRYNLEY

Oklahoma, USA

HELPING HANDS

"EVERYONE
DESERVES TO
BE HAPPY."

Did you know that being kind to others releases chemicals in our brains that make us feel happy and puts us in a good mood? One single act of kindness is good for you, but in order to make the effects last, you need to make acts of kindness a regular practice, which is exactly what Brynley Meade does.

For Brynley's fifth birthday, she chose to donate toys to a local hospital instead of getting gifts for herself. Her mother put a note in her party invitations and posted her idea on social media. Family and friends responded generously. Brynley was excited to donate the gifts to the children at the hospital.

A CRISIS NURSERY is a place where families who are having an emergency can take their children for short-term care.

For her sixth birthday, Brynley wanted to do it again, but this time she wanted to let in-need children choose their own toys. Her mother called the local **crisis nursery** and arranged for Brynley to donate toys. She personally gave a toy to every child there.

Then when she turned seven, Brynley decided to donate Christmas trees to nursing homes. Because of COVID, most nursing homes were locked down and the residents were lonely. Brynley wanted to make sure everyone had Christmas decorations to cheer them up. COVID

BRYNLEY'S FUN FACTS:

- Her favorite food is chicken with gravy.
- She loves to play Uno.
- Brynley's favorite colors are purple, pink, and turquoise.
- Her favorite animals are bunnies.

prevented Brynley from having a birthday party, but through the power of social media, Amazon wish lists, and the help of her family and friends, Brynley reached her goal of eighty trees, one for each resident in a local long-term care center.

Brynley plans to donate more toys for her next birthday, and to continue helping people.

- **Make a goal of doing at least one act of kindness every day.**

- **Try to get into the habit of being kind to others. Smile, help without being asked, speak kind words, hold the door and more!**

- **Check out this website for ideas: www.kindness.org**

An **ACT OF KINDNESS** makes the other person feel important or recognized, especially at a time when they might be feeling sad or lonely.

BRYNLEY'S ADVICE FOR YOU:
Everyone can be a helper. Always be kind.

Brynley

ASHER

California, USA

INSPIRATIONAL ICONS

"YOU ALWAYS NEED TO BELIEVE IN YOURSELF."

Do you have a favorite sport? Have you ever dreamt, or know anyone who's dreamt, of being in the Olympics?

That is Asher's goal.

Asher Loena was born with spina bifida, which means his spine and spinal cord didn't form properly. He wears braces to walk, but uses a wheelchair to travel longer distances.

When Asher was 18 months old, his mother saw a flyer about a disability sports festival in their area. She brought Asher there, and he had the opportunity to try many different sports. At the festival his mother met Clayton French, the founder of **Angel City Sports**, and his son Ezra, an amputee who made the USA **Paralympic** team for high jump. Ezra became a huge inspiration for Asher. At the age

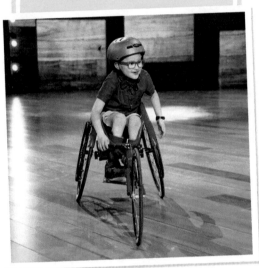

ADAPTIVE SPORTS: Competitive or recreational sports for people with disabilities.

ANGEL CITY SPORTS: Provides year-round free adaptive sports opportunities for kids, adults, and veterans with physical disabilities or visual impairments.

THE PARALYMPICS: A series of international contests for athletes with disabilities that are held following the summer and winter Olympic Games.

of five, Asher competed in his first **adaptive sports** competition with Angel City Sports. It was then that he met his coach, Paralympian and gold medal winner Candace Cable. She saw his determination and focus and was excited to work with him. Asher has since tried many sports including basketball, swimming, shot put, javelin, golf and tennis. He is classified as a seated athlete (competing from his wheelchair), which means he can't compete any other way and does not do any jumping sports. Of the sports he's tried, his favorites are wheelchair racing, wheelchair tennis, and golf.

Having people in his life that have achieved lofty sports goals has pushed Asher to be his very best. In turn, Asher encourages younger athletes. He cheers on the other athletes he plays with, even his own competitors. Asher also encourages people to see that just because he has different abilities does not mean he can't play the same sports as everyone else. He has spoken at his school and in his classroom about his love of adaptive sports.

Being involved in the adaptive sports community and seeing athletes compete has given Asher strength and hope. Now, he hopes he can encourage other kids to go for their dreams, too.

BECOME A young CHANGEMAKERS™ INSPIRATIONAL ICON!

- **Don't be afraid to push yourself out of your comfort zone and try new things!**
- **Go after your dreams— don't give up.**

ASHER'S ADVICE FOR YOU:
Be confident, be brave and believe in yourself.

Asher

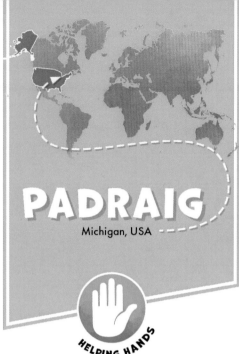

PADRAIG

Michigan, USA

HELPING HANDS

"LET'S DO THIS!"

Did you know that around the world, about 690 million people regularly go to bed hungry every night? Many people can't afford to eat nutritious food on a daily basis. Maybe you've experienced not knowing where your next meal is coming from, or know someone who has.

You may not think you can do anything to help fill people's bellies, but Padraig Baron wants to tell you that you can! When Padraig was just two years old, he watched his mother help feed the homeless in Detroit. Right then and there, he decided he wanted to help, too! He took a small, but very important, step and asked his mom to buy granola bars to keep in the car. He wanted to hand them out himself through the car window.

That was just the beginning. Helping others became a way of life for Padraig. In 2020, during the COVID-19 pandemic, Padraig and his mother's nonprofit organization Frugal On The Fly signed up to distribute food boxes from the USDA's Farm to Families program. They passed the food out to neighbors in need at a local plaza parking lot. They began with 25 families, but quickly ran out of food. Padraig encouraged his mother to pick up more food to pass out.

Their Frugal On The Fly "Free Food Fridays" quickly grew and soon they were giving 250 families free produce each week. They saw firsthand how the pandemic was affecting families. Some people found themselves in a food line for the very first time in their lives.

Padraig inspired his friends and family to jump in as volunteers. This resulted in a volunteer team

PADRAIG'S FUN FACTS:

- Padraig enjoys hockey.
- He loves ice cream cones with sprinkles.
- He likes science.

of about forty people who served anywhere between 1,500 and 3,500 families weekly. The team ended up passing out one million pounds of fresh, nutritious food in 23 weeks!

Padraig's community outreach didn't stop there. He donated his books to Little Free Libraries in his neighbor-hood. With public libraries closed, he wanted to make sure kids had access to new books.

Padraig gathered used coats and hats from family and neighbors, and helped a local coat drive get warm winter gear to people in need.

Helping out people in his community is important to Padraig; it makes his heart happy. Padraig dreams of being president one day. He wants to make the world a better place for everyone!

BECOME A young CHANGEMAKERS™ HELPING HAND!

- **Visit www.frugalonthefly.com to learn more about Padraig's mission.**

- **Visit www.foodrescue.us to read more about food rescue in the United States.**

- **Go through your clothes, books and toys. Donate them to a local shelter.**

PADRAIG'S ADVICE FOR YOU:

If you can't find organizations allowing kid volunteers, start your own projects. You can do something by yourself and still make a difference. Then, get your friends involved. One person can make a difference.

ANABELLE

New York, USA

ANIMAL AMBASSADORS

"HELPING ANIMALS IS
THE BEST GIFT OF ALL."

Anabelle Abrams has always had a soft spot in her heart for animals. One Christmas, when she was seven years old, Anabelle was feeling sad for all of the animals who were alone over the holidays. That inspired her to take action.

Since Anabelle's birthday is December 18, she and her mom decided to put a note inside of her birthday invitations asking for pet supplies to be donated instead of birthday gifts. Anabelle was amazed and overwhelmed by the response and generosity of her family and friends. She delivered all of the supplies to the local animal shelter that helps place abandoned or orphaned animals into their forever homes. For Anabelle, one of the most enjoyable parts of the donation was putting all of the supplies under the shelter's Christmas tree.

Anabelle has since turned this into an annual tradition. Every year on her birthday, Anabelle collects donations instead of gifts, then drops the supplies off at the shelter. She loves knowing that the animals will get Christmas presents, too. And of course she loves the chance to hold and cuddle the animals! Anabelle plans to continue her yearly tradition, and hopes to collect more supplies each year. She also plans to have a "LemonARF" stand to sell lemonade, and will donate the proceeds to the animal shelter. When she's older, Anabelle wants to volunteer at the shelter and foster some kittens.

ANABELLE'S FUN FACTS:

- Her family has a friendly deer that visits their house named Tick Tick.

- Her family fostered and adopted two kitties.

- She loves reading *Percy Jackson* and Greek mythology.

BECOME A young CHANGEMAKERS™ 🐾 ANIMAL AMBASSADOR!

Find an animal shelter in your area. Can you volunteer there? Do they need supplies? Find out what you can do to help!

ANABELLE'S ADVICE FOR YOU:

Making a difference is all about finding something that matters to you and your community and trying to make it better. If we all try, this world could be a better place.

Anabelle 🐾

CHRISTIAN

Connecticut, USA

HELPING HANDS

"BE PART OF THE RIPPLE EFFECT. SPREAD KINDNESS."

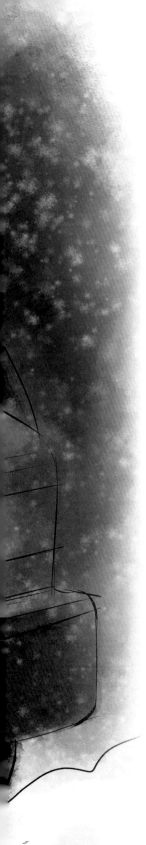

Have you ever seen one small act of kindness change someone's entire day? Maybe you held the door for someone at the store, gave someone who looked lonely a smile, or helped someone carry a heavy box? Christian Stone and his mother have always believed that being kind to others is one of the most important things you can do.

During the height of the COVID-19 pandemic, Christian's community experienced heavy snowfall. Christian knew the doctors, nurses, and other staff at the local hospital were working overtime to help those who were sick. He wanted to do something that would help ease their burden. After brainstorming with his family, Christian decided to clear the snow off of vehicle windshields in the parking lot.

Although it was challenging getting the vehicles cleaned off during a blizzard, seeing the smiles and looks of relief on the healthcare workers' faces when they came out after a long day of work made it worth it. The workers were happy to be able to get into their warm cars and leave right away to get home to their families.

Christian helps people whenever he can. He picks things up when people drop them, helps people carry stuff, and holds doors for people. Because he loves animals, he wants to help them in the future. He hopes to encourage you to get out there and do an act of kindness for someone. You never know what people are going through. Your small act of kindness has the power to change lives.

BECOME A

young CHANGEMAKERS™ HELPING HAND!

CHRISTIAN'S ADVICE FOR YOU:

One small act of kindness could change someone's entire day. We are the next generation of leaders, let's get out there and do an act of kindness today.

- **Look for ways to help the people around you: rake a neighbor's yard, bring someone flowers, help your family without being asked.**

- **Make a goal of doing at least one act of kindness each day.**

Christian

ADA

West Yorkshire, England

INSPIRATIONAL ICONS

"I LOVE RUNNING AND
RAISING PENNIES FOR CLDF."

Ada Butterfield was born with a rare, and often fatal, type of liver disease called biliary atresia, in which the **bile ducts** are clogged. Bile is a fluid made by the liver, an organ that gets rid of waste. Usually the bile travels from the liver to the small intestines, but in Ada's case, it was getting backed up, which damaged her liver.

At five weeks old, Ada had a life-saving operation, and although it helped, she will need check-ups and medication for the rest of her life. Ada may even need a new liver one day. When the Children's Liver Disease Foundation (CLDF) learned about Ada, they quickly stepped up to help her and her family and give them hope and support.

Since then, Ada has done her best to give back. When a marathon her mom was planning to run in April 2020 was cancelled because of the COVID-19 pandemic, Ada decided to create her own running event. Better yet, she used that opportunity to raise money for the charity that had given them so much support. Her family spread the word on social media and planned a route through Ada's neighborhood. Ada's friends lined the streets and cheered her on. She raised over $4,000 for CLDF with this one event alone!

ADA'S FUN FACTS:

- Ada loves cabbage.
- Ada is a night owl—she loves staying up late.
- Her favorite people are her cousins, Eliza and Violet.

Through this fundraiser, Ada found her own love of running–and of giving back. Ada set a goal to run twenty miles over the course of a month. Her parents used social media to let people know that she would be doing this challenge and people started donating in Ada's name. Inspired by Ada, over 230 other kids decided to join her in running for charity!

Ada and her parents have raised over $68,000 for the charity so far and have no plans to stop fundraising any time soon.

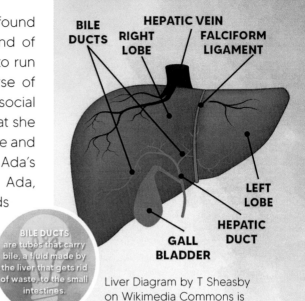

BILE DUCTS
RIGHT LOBE
HEPATIC VEIN
FALCIFORM LIGAMENT
LEFT LOBE
HEPATIC DUCT
GALL BLADDER

BILE DUCTS are tubes that carry bile, a fluid made by the liver that gets rid of waste, to the small intestines.

Liver Diagram by T Sheasby on Wikimedia Commons is licensed under CC BY-SA 3.0. Labels adjusted.

BECOME A young CHANGEMAKERS™ INSPIRATIONAL ICON!

Donate to Ada's cause at:
www.childliverdisease.org

● **Find a way to raise money to donate to charity.**

LET'S LEARN ABOUT THE LIVER!

Your liver is an organ with many important jobs including:

- Cleaning your blood.

- Producing an important digestive liquid called bile.

- Storing energy in the form of a sugar called glycogen.

ADA'S ADVICE FOR YOU:
Just do it, it makes you feel good and happy!

C.J.
Georgia, USA

HELPING HANDS

BLANKIES
4
MY BUDDIES

blankis 4 my buddies

"The blankets I give aren't merely presents, they are more about presence and letting children know that someone cares about them. I was once a kid experiencing something hard– the grief of losing a sibling– and just having the support of my family and a comfy blanket made me feel safe."

After losing his baby sister when he was just five years old, C.J. Matthews was inspired to do something to help other kids healing from traumatic situations. Since blankets have always been one of his favorite things, he decided to raise money to buy blankets and donate them to kids in need of comfort.

"I wanted to give kids something that was a symbol of security and made them feel safe. Blankets wrap around you like a hug."

C.J. and his family ran a GoFundMe campaign so family and friends across the country could contribute. They also teamed up with a friend to host a drop-off event at her place of business. Local newspapers advertised for the event, and people

NICU stands for Newborn Intensive Care Unit. This is a nursery in a hospital that provides around-the-clock care to sick or premature babies (babies born early).

donated more than 600 blankets! Many of the blankets donated were throw blankets, but members from a local mom's group gave crocheted and other handmade blankets. Those were used as a special donation to babies in the NICU in honor of C.J.'s baby sister.

As much as C.J. liked the idea of donating blankets, what he really wanted was to make sure the blankets got to the kids who needed them. He and his family contacted local hospitals, orphan relief centers, group homes, and different types of shelters (homeless, emergency, domestic violence, and those for teen moms).

C.J. and his family turned their collection event into an annual

C.J.'s Fun Facts:

- He is afraid of most bugs!
- Gumbo is his favorite food.
- C.J.'s dog Bentley is older than he is, and he has two turtles–one of which he's had since he was four years old.

23 ✋

winter tradition and called it Blankies 4 My Buddies.

But C.J. didn't stop with donated blankets. He also helps kids make do-it-yourself (DIY) blankets through a program he started called Give like C.J. Participants receive a DIY blanket kit, with which they can make a special custom blanket to share with someone they know or even a stranger who is in need of comfort.

C.J.'s future plans include expanding his project to help even more people on a larger scale. He is developing his own line of blankets and other products! His ultimate goal is to create a social impact company that donates one blanket to a child in need for every blanket that is purchased.

C.J. wants you to know that you're never too young or too old to use your voice to make a difference in the world!

- **Talk to your family about supporting underserved kids in your area.**
- **Be kind to people–you never know what someone else is going through.**
- **Visit C.J.'s website to see how you can help!**
  www.blankies4mybuddies.org

C.J.'S ADVICE FOR YOU:

Just do it. It doesn't matter how big or small your idea is–any act of kindness matters and goes a long way. My mom always reminds me that people will forget what you say or do, but will always remember how you made them feel. A genuine act of kindness from a friend or a stranger will always be remembered.

C.J.

SHARLEEN

California, USA

"ANYONE CAN MAKE A DIFFERENCE IN THE WORLD— DREAM BIG AND KEEP INNOVATING!"

Sharleen Loh has been curious about the world around her since she was a young child. Her parents fueled her natural curiosity by bringing her to STEM fairs. STEM stands for Science, Technology, Engineering, and Mathematics. It helps explain how and why things work, how to invent things, and how to solve problems. For Sharleen, STEM fairs were love at first sight. She couldn't get enough of the experiments and was always asking questions about how and why the experiments turned out the way they did.

As she got older, she wondered why other kids her age didn't share the same love of STEM. She remembered all of the fun STEM activities she was exposed to as a child and decided to try to make STEM programs available to kids who didn't have access to them.

As she researched STEM, Sharleen learned that not only were the experiments cool, but STEM education improves creative thinking, encourages teamwork, and helps children develop communication skills–an important life skill. It also empowers critical thinking, improves social skills, and boosts curiosity.

SHARLEEN'S FUN FACTS:

- **In kindergarten, her dream job was to be a "pizza lady"!**

- **Her favorite food is a dessert that her grandmother loved to make for her throughout childhood: 湯圓 (tāngyuán)–sweet, chewy rice balls served in soup.**

- **In her free time, she loves crocheting little stuffed animals (amigurumi) for her friends and family.**

UNDERPRIVILEGED children don't have the advantages other children have. They usually live in poverty.

When she was 13 years old, Sharleen approached the principal and PTA (Parent-Teacher Association) at her school, who agreed to let her host a STEM night. She spent nine months researching and planning the event, which over 700 people attended. It was so successful and she got so much positive feedback that her principal turned it into an annual event!

A few weeks later, Sharleen initiated the first STEM program at a local club where **underprivileged** children went after school. She designed her STEM activities around hands-on experimentation, involvement, and fun! This allowed children to explore their natural curiosity. Eventually, attendance in her program grew and she had to recruit volunteers (whom she calls STEMbers) to help.

Sharleen turned her program into the non-profit organization STEMup4Youth and started receiving invitations to host large STEM events. To keep up with the requests, she recruited more STEMbers and formed chapters of STEMup4Youth. Today, there are 15 chapters and 4 divisions reaching 50,000 children around the world! Her goal is to continue to inspire children around the world to be excited about and pursue STEM.

BECOME A young CHANGEMAKERS™ INSPIRATIONAL ICON!

- **Get curious: what do you wonder about? Write some ideas down, then try to find the answers.**

- **Visit www.stemup4youth. com for more information about Sharleen's program.**

- **Push yourself out of your comfort zone. Don't be afraid to try something new.**

SHARLEEN'S ADVICE FOR YOU:
Anyone can make a difference in the world–dream big and keep innovating!

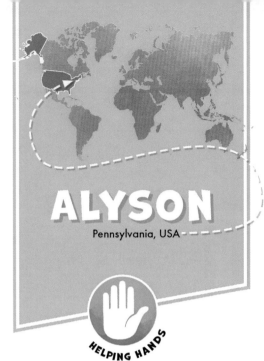

ALYSON

Pennsylvania, USA

HELPING HANDS

"CHANGING THE WORLD, ONE MONKEY AT A TIME."

Is there something special that makes you feel better when you're sick? Maybe it's a person, a pet, a book, a special meal, or a toy. For Alyson, it was a stuffed monkey.

When Alyson Creasy was eight years old, she was hospitalized with an illness. While in the emergency room, her grandmother gave her a stuffed monkey to comfort her. Having something to hold on to did make Aly feel better, and she was inspired to help other children in the same way.

Aly decided that since it was a stuffed monkey that comforted her, she would give stuffed monkeys to other kids in the hospital. She sat down with her family to figure out how to achieve her goal. She created a spreadsheet with goals of how many monkeys she wanted to be able to donate. Then, she started to share her vision with people. Aly's community came together and helped her raise money. She began with simple "monkey drops" at area hospitals, but slowly began to grow those monkey drops. Around the same time, Aly received a note from a family who had read about her movement. Their young daughter, Olivia, had passed away, and they were looking for a charity to support in her memory. Aly knew at once what to do.

HOSPITAL

She worked with a local company to create a unique monkey she could donate, and she named it "The Olivia Monkey." Now, Aly's Monkey Movement sends an average of 200 monkeys out per month!

Aly's Monkey Movement has expanded to provide a more personal service, too-it gives people the opportunity to personally request monkeys for specific people. Aly and her siblings tag and name each monkey according to the sponsor's name or request before they are sent to their forever homes. The tag invites the recipient and their monkey to share a photo on Aly's Facebook page. This gives the community the opportunity to meet the children they sponsor.

Aly's movement is growing by the day, and is full of positive supporters who rally around these families with love, encouragement, and guidance. Together Aly hopes they can change the world, one monkey at a time.

ALY'S FUN FACTS:

- She's afraid of spiders!
- Aly loves basketball.
- She loves doing magic tricks.

BECOME A young CHANGEMAKERS™ HELPING HAND!

- Do something kind for children in a hospital near you. Make cards or colorful posters.

- Visit www.alysmonkeys.org to find out how to request a monkey for someone in need.

- Donate toward Aly's cause!

ALY'S ADVICE FOR YOU:
Be a leader, not a follower–unless you're following your heart!

Aly

RYAN

Ontario, Canada

CONSERVATION CREW

"LET'S ALL DO OUR PART TO MAKE THE WORLD A BETTER PLACE."

Do you have a favorite teacher? One who has inspired and encouraged you? One who has even changed your life?

Ryan Hreljac's first grade teacher changed his. One day, she told him that people were sick and dying because they didn't have access to clean drinking water. She explained that some people had to walk miles each day to get water, and sometimes it was just to get dirty water. Something stirred in Ryan's heart, and he decided to take action. He did odd jobs around the house to earn money to buy a well for a school in Uganda. He earned $70 and thought that would be enough. It turned out he needed $2,000 for the well. Ryan knew he needed the help of others, so he began speaking in public. He made his first speech at seven years old. He spoke at clubs, schools... anywhere that would have him so he could raise money

to build that well. It took him about a year, but he raised the $2,000.

Once Ryan had raised enough money to drill the well, one of his neighbors donated air miles so Ryan could travel to Uganda to see it for himself. Over 500 people in the community lined up to welcome Ryan and his family to Uganda. There was a huge party–a feast, singing, clapping–all because they had clean water. It was humbling for Ryan. Like many children, he took for granted that he had access to clean water any time he wanted it. During that visit, he met his penpal, Jimmy, who later became a part of Ryan's family through adoption (Jimmy's parents disappeared during the country's civil war).

Ryan came home from his trip motivated to do more. He'd seen firsthand how bad the water situation was, and he wanted to keep helping, so he went back to fundraising. By the second year, he had raised $61,000. In 2001, he founded Ryan's Well Foundation in order to keep bringing clean water and sanitation to people who needed it.

Ryan's foundation started with building wells, but in 2005 they began building latrines, too. The latrines that his foundation builds provide a safe way for people to get rid of their waste so their drinking water isn't dirty–an important change to their lifestyle because dirty drinking water causes infection and disease. Ryan's foundation also teaches kids good hand washing hygiene so they can keep themselves and their communities safe, clean, and healthy.

Ryan's foundation has completed over 1,500 water projects and 1,200 latrines in 17 countries, bringing safe water and sanitation to over a million people!

BECOME A

CONSERVATION CREW MEMBER!

LATRINE: A toilet or outhouse that the whole community uses.

- **Research more about helping the over one billion people who don't have access to clean drinking water.**

- **Visit www.ryanswell.ca to learn more about Ryan's foundation and how you can help!**

RYAN'S FUN FACTS:

- Ryan loves to read.

- He enjoys camping.

- His favorite place is Uganda, Africa.

- His least favorite food is eggplant.

RYAN'S ADVICE FOR YOU:

In order to make a positive change in the world, you need to find something you are passionate about and then you need to take steps to act.

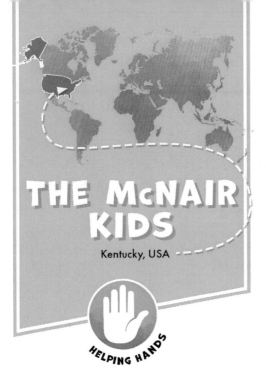

THE McNAIR KIDS
Kentucky, USA

HELPING HANDS

"EVERY PERSON HAS A NAME, EVERY NAME HAS A STORY, AND EVERY SINGLE STORY MATTERS TO GOD."

—IAN

"MISSIONS HELP PEOPLE WHO RELY MOSTLY ON YOU TO HELP THEM GET THROUGH THE YEAR. PLAY WITH CHICKENS SECOND, DO THE WORK FIRST!"

—NATE

Have you ever gone on a mission trip, or do you know someone who has? Ian, Nate, Clara, and Livy McNair wanted to help people living in Haiti, a very poor island nation in the Caribbean which has suffered from many hurricanes.

Because their church supports an orphanage there, the family was given an opportunity to go on a mission trip – a trip where people spend time helping those in need.

Although only older brothers Ian and Nate were able to go on the trip (with their father), Clara and Livy helped, too, by drawing pictures and selling them to collect money for the people of Haiti.

When they arrived, the boys were shocked to find that the orphanage did not have electricity, indoor plumbing, or air conditioning. With so little space, the orphans slept in beds stacked on top of each other. There were between six and eight kids per room, with separate buildings for the boys and girls. They were also surprised to find that the kids didn't have toys, which meant the children had to create fun out of whatever they could find–including chickens!

Ian and Nate knew they couldn't solve all of the orphanage's problems, but they wanted to do what they could. They helped repair the school and medical buildings at the orphanage, and helped their dad build a water collection gutter system, since the Haitians don't have clean drinking water.

Seeing how other people live made Ian and Nate more grateful for what they have. It upset them to see that not all kids have a good life. They want to go back someday to help again, especially Nate, who wants to be a doctor one day. He would like to see how their hospitals work without modern equipment to better understand how he can help. Clara and Livy hope to go when they are old enough.

Florida, USA

Haiti

HAITI is in the western one-third of the island of Hispaniola between the Caribbean Sea and the North Atlantic Ocean. Haiti is the poorest country in the Latin American and Caribbean region, and among the poorest countries in the world.

35

young CHANGEMAKERS™ HELPING HAND!

- Raise money for a charity that you love: set up lemonade stands. Have a bake sale. Have a carwash with your friends.

- Look for ways to volunteer in your community.

- Look into taking a mission trip with your family.

THEIR ADVICE FOR YOU:

You don't have to travel overseas to make a difference. You can find a local charity to support right in your own community.

Livy Ian Nate Clara♡

FUN FACTS ABOUT THE KIDS:

- Livy likes dance, art, and gymnastics. She was adopted from the Congo.

- Ian loves soccer and enjoyed playing it with the Haitian children who love it as well.

- Nate plans to be a doctor and wants to study infectious disease.

- Clara hopes to grow up and train service dogs. She enjoys making slime and dog treats.

ZURIEL

California, USA

Did you know that there are 16.7 million girls out of school in **Sub-Saharan Africa**, 9.3 million of whom will never set foot in a classroom? Millions of girls worldwide are not able to attend school, partially because of poverty and partially because in some countries educating girls is not considered important.

In many cases, families can't afford the fees they must pay in order for their children to attend school. Some families even force their daughters to marry at young ages so they will have one less mouth to feed.

Zuriel Oduwole wants to change that. Born in California, United States, Zuriel's dad's side of the family is from Nigeria, Africa. At nine years old Zuriel entered a competition through her school to create a documentary about a historical **revolution**. Many of her classmates chose to feature revolutions in the United States and Asian countries. Because of her African roots, Zuriel decided to do a documentary based there. Through her research, Zuriel learned that the Ghana revolution was one of the most successful held on the continent. She was able to visit Ghana to do research on the project. During that trip, she wondered why the girls were selling things on the streets instead of being in school. She also learned that girls as young as six

years old have to make bricks to sell to help their families instead of going to school. She talked to her parents about it not being fair, and they challenged her to do something about it. She took action, writing to the presidents of different African countries (Kenya, Liberia, Malawi), asking to speak to them about girls staying in school.

Many people didn't take Zuriel seriously at first because of her age, but her parents and siblings encouraged her to keep going. They reminded her of all of the girls who would be inspired and helped by what she wanted to do.

Since then, Zuriel has spoken to more than 50,000 youths worldwide, especially in countries such as Tanzania, Egypt, Nigeria, Ghana, South Africa, and Kenya about the power of education and believing in your dreams—especially if you want to change your community.

Zuriel has also spoken with over 31 presidents and world leaders, many in Africa, about making policies that enable girls to go to school until at least the age of 18

NORTH AFRICA

SUB-SAHARAN AFRICA

SUB-SAHARAN AFRICA: The area of the continent of Africa that lies south of the Sahara.

A **REVOLUTION** occurs when people decide to take power from a government that treats them unfairly.

so they don't have to get married when they are 12 or 13. One of her biggest successes was in 2019 when Mozambique formally outlawed child marriage.

Zuriel also founded Dream Up, Speak Up, Stand Up (DUSUSU), a charity that advocates for girls' education. DUSUSU also recognizes and awards African first ladies for their work to promote girls' education.

Zuriel hopes that through this mission, she can be a voice for change.

Zuriel is shaking hands with President Filipe Nyusi of Mozambique, a country that formally outlawed child marriage in 2019.

BECOME A

young CHANGEMAKERS™ INSPIRATIONAL ICON!

- **What do you love? Plants? Animals? Kids? Find an organization that works for the good of them! Write a letter to someone who has the power to help.**

- **Learn about Zuriel's charity: www.dususu.org**

ZURIEL'S ADVICE FOR YOU:

You're young, so people might not take you seriously at first, but don't stop. Keep fighting for what you believe in.

Zuriel

ZURIEL'S FUN FACTS:

- **She would like to be president of the United States.**

- **She likes to play soccer and basketball.**

- **Zuriel is very close to her family—they enjoy watching old detective television shows.**

- **She likes going shopping and to the beach with her friends.**

STACY C. BAUER

A native of Minneapolis, MN, Stacy C. Bauer is a wife, teacher, mother of two and owner of Hop Off the Press–a publisher of quality children's books. Along with self publishing her own books, Stacy enjoys helping aspiring authors realize their dreams. She is hoping to inspire people around the world to make a difference with her newest endeavor, nonfiction book series *Young Change Makers*. For more information and to check out Stacy's other books including her children's picture books, visit www.stacycbauer.com.

EMANUELA NTAMACK

Emanuela Ntamack is an artist and children's book illustrator, a beloved wife and mother. She is married to her Cameroonian husband Alix, and together they have two boys. She has been drawing continuously ever since she could hold a pencil. Growing up, she studied Art and Design in school and university. After she became a mother, she discovered her love for children's books illustrations. One of the biggest satisfactions of her work is when children–including her own–are inspired by the illustrations that she creates. She is thankful to God for the gift of art, and for the diversity and the beauty of Creation, which is a never-ending source of inspiration.